All About
Julia Morgan

To Addi —
Julia Morgan was a very talented lady and she lived at the same time as your Great-great-great Grandmother, Julia Morgan, who came west on a flatboat on the Ohio River with her mother at age 10 years.

Your mom is named after her.

Phyllis J. Perry

Love,
Mimi ♡
☺

BLUE RIVER PRESS
Indianapolis, Indiana

Contents

All About
Julia Morgan

Preface

Julia Morgan lived an extraordinary life. In the field of architecture, she was a true pioneer, exploring areas almost unknown to women of her time. In 1894, she was the first woman to graduate from the University of California, Berkeley, with a Bachelor of Science degree in civil engineering. In 1898, she became the first woman to be accepted into the architecture program at the world-famous École nationale supérieure des Beaux-Arts in Paris and, on completion of the program, earned her certificate in 1901. In 1904, she was the first woman to receive an architect's license from the State of California.

Morgan pushed boundaries and refused to accept the barriers and constraints on women that were common at the time she lived. More than a pioneering woman, she also created more than 700 buildings, many of which still stand as a testimony to her art and skill. Julia Morgan is believed to have said, "My buildings will be my legacy. . . they will speak for me after I'm gone."

The towers of La Casa Grande were inspired by the tower of the cathedral in Ronda, Spain (shown on page 75).

Some of these buildings are well known, like Hearst Castle at San Simeon, the conference center at Asilomar, the Bavarian-style cottages at Wyntoon, and the bell tower and library at Mills College in Oakland, California. Others are less well known such as the arts and crafts style house in the Sierra Nevadas built for the manager of the North Star Mine near Grass Valley, California. She also built houses, churches, hospitals, schools, auditoriums, gymnasiums, and many buildings for the YWCA.

To each project, big and small, she brought dedication and a determination to meet the wishes of her clients. Julia worked constantly at her craft while finding time to assist other young architects, many of whom were women, to get their start in the field of architecture.

Hats were a way for women in the Victorian era, when Julia Morgan grew up, to show their social standing.

Chapter 1

Julia Morgan's Childhood

In 1848, gold was discovered at Sutter's Fort in California. As news of this discovery spread, the gold rush began. Among the thousands of people who flocked from the east to the west to seek their fortunes was Julia Morgan's father, Charles Bill Morgan. He had been a mining engineer in New York, and he was eager to go to California and try to make a fortune in the gold fields there.

It was in 1867 that Bill Morgan made his first trip west from Connecticut. Such a journey at that time was a great adventure. Like many others during the gold rush, he reached California by boat, going around the tip of South America and then sailing north to the fabled city of San Francisco. He wanted to take a good look at the Golden State to see if this was the place for him to settle.

Charles Morgan, Julia's father, was a mining engineer, meaning he planned how, when, and where to mine, but wasn't actually a miner himself.

Bill was not disappointed. He found many mining corporations were opening in California, and with his knowledge and experience in mining engineering, he was sure he would find a good job. Small in stature, Bill was a friendly, outgoing man. He loved San Francisco, and decided this was where he wanted to live and raise his family.

He returned to the east just long enough to marry Eliza Parmalee. Although he had announced his plans to take his bride to San Francisco and told his in-laws what a lovely city it was, the Parmalees had their doubts. To them, San Francisco sounded like the wild west.

Eliza Parmalee's father, Albert Parmalee, was a rich man who had made his money as a cotton trader. He and his wife didn't like the thought of their pampered daughter, who tended to be quiet and reserved, being so far away. They thought of California as the rough frontier. Before Charles and Eliza left for California, Eliza's father gave her money and promised to give more whenever she needed it. In the years that followed, he made good on that promise. Although Bill Morgan worked at many jobs, he was never a tremendous success and did not amass a fortune as he had dreamed.

At first, Bill and Eliza Morgan lived in San Francisco on Market Street in the Palace Hotel.

Eliza Parmalee, Julia's mother, was a wealthy socialite
who was very confident and independent
and taught Julia to be the same way.

During the day, Bill was at work and Eliza was
busy taking care of their apartment. In 1870, a
son, Parmalee, was born to them, and then on
January 20, 1872, they had a daughter, Julia.

With two children to raise, Charles and Eliza
Morgan decided it was time to leave their rented
apartment. They built a house across the bay

from San Francisco in the town of Oakland. Oakland was a quieter town than San Francisco and was already filled with homes and churches. Bill Morgan bought a lot at the north end of the city in 1872.

Julia's childhood home was typical of the Victorian era and held many rooms with specific functions.

The Morgans built a three-story Victorian house that was large enough for all of them. In the style of the time, the house had a large front living room and dining room filled with heavy drapes and fancy Victorian furniture. Julia had a large bedroom on the second floor. There were also rooms above theirs for the maid and the cook.

Eliza was happy with the children in their new house. Bill Morgan rode a ferry across the bay to his office each morning. He tried many different jobs. He was a sugar broker, he invested in stores, and he bought stock in an unsuccessful gold mine. He served on commissions and was the Director of the Oakland Public Schools. Bill became part owner in a company that made steam powered tractors.

Bill was not very successful at any of his many business pursuits. Eliza used money from her father to help run her household in Oakland and to raise their growing family. After Parmalee and Julia were born, Emma, Avery, and Gardner Bulkley (called Sam by his family and friends) joined the family. Each time a new baby arrived, Eliza's father sent more money. His daughter would return home for a visit to have the babies baptized in New York. Eliza and her children would ride east on the recently completed transcontinental railroad.

In the summer of 1878, Eliza and her children went to visit her family in New York. This time,

As a child, Julia didn't like sitting still for photos and would rather have been playing with her brothers.

they stayed for a year, enjoying the comfort of Eliza's father's house. Eliza and the children returned to Oakland in the summer of 1879. There Julia caught a cold that developed into an infection in the bones behind her ear. Without the medicines that are available today, this was a serious illness. Some people with serious ear infections became deaf or even died. It took a long time for Julia to recover. An ear problem affected Julia all her life.

After her illness, Julia's parents wanted to protect her and keep her quiet, but Julia was not a quiet child. As she grew, Julia preferred to play with her brothers rather than with her sister, Emma. Although small, Julia was strong and had a lot of stamina. She was active and always on the go. She liked to play on her brothers' gym equipment and took up archery. It was one of the few sports at that time which was considered "proper" for young girls.

Around this time, the first female architect in the United States opened her first office. Louise Blanchard was born in Waterloo, New York in 1856. She graduated from Buffalo Central High School in 1874. Instead of going to college to learn to be an architect, she took a job drafting in an architect's office and studied on her own. In 1881, on opening her office in Buffalo, New York, Louise became the first professional female architect in the United States. That same year, she married architect, Robert Bethune. After two years, they had their only child and hired a third architect who became their partner in the firm.

In twenty-two years in business, Bethune's firm built fifteen commercial buildings, eight industrial buildings, and several schools. Among these buildings were a prison, a church, and a baseball facility. The impressive Hotel Lafayette, completed in 1904, was considered to be her masterpiece.

In 1888, Bethune became the first woman admitted to the American Institute of Architects. She was also active in campaigning for more women and better pay for women in the field of architecture.

Bethune retired in 1908 and died in 1913.

Like Louise, Julia was fascinated with mechanical things. When she thought about what she wanted to be when she grew up, Julia thought she might want to enter the medical field. She was interested in being a doctor, although at that time there were very few female doctors. She, her siblings, and the children of their wealthy neighbors all attended Riverside Grammar School and then Oakland High School.

For summer vacations, the Morgans often went to the California seashore. Sometimes they went to Santa Cruz, and other times they went to Catalina Island. Some years they would make the trip back to the east coast to visit relatives there. While on one of these trips to New York, Julia saw the newly built Brooklyn Bridge. One of her cousins, Lucy Thornton, was married to Pierre LeBrun, an architect. LeBrun had built the Metropolitan Life Insurance Tower in New York City. He praised Julia for her ability in mathematics and drawing. Perhaps her interest

The Brooklyn Bridge was originally designed by Washington Roebling, but after he got sick, his wife Emily took over supervising the bridge's construction.

in becoming an architect started then.

Julia loved school and did very well. She took subjects such as advanced math, Latin, and German, in addition to taking lessons after school in dancing, violin, and piano. Julia's sister, Emma, also did very well in school, while their brothers were only average students.

As the Morgan children grew up, so did the cities of Oakland and San Francisco. Julia would go for walks with her family in Oakland and look at the rapidly growing neighborhoods filled with half-built houses. They had once lived at the edge of town, but as Oakland grew, they found themselves closer to the center of town. Across the bay, San Francisco grew into a great city with large buildings and a busy port.

As a high school student, Julia considered a career in medicine for a short time because it had appealed to her as a child. Julia was also attracted to the field of architecture. She thought she might like to build structures like Pierre LeBrun did in New York. LeBrun encouraged this interest and wrote letters to young Julia Morgan.

When she was eighteen and a senior in Oakland High School, Julia told her mother

Julia and her siblings attended Oakland High School, which was built in 1872.

that she did not want a party or to become a fashionable lady. She did not want a purely social life in which her main object would be to look for a husband. Instead, she wanted to go to college. Julia's mother was very supportive of her. In many ways, the two were alike, each being shy and quiet. Her mother encouraged Julia's plans for a future as a professional architect.

Sather Gate marks the entrance
to the University of California in Berkeley.

In 1873, the University of California opened in Berkeley, now called UC Berkeley. The University was close to home, and Julia wanted to go to school there. So in 1890, after graduating from high school and gaining her mother's support, Julia enrolled at the UC Berkeley.

At almost the same time that Julia was applying to enter the UC Berkeley, a female architect made headlines across the United States. Sophia Hayden, who was the first woman to get a degree in architecture at the Massachusetts Institute of Technology, won a competition to design the exterior of a Woman's Building for the World's Fair to be held in Chicago in 1892. Hayden was only four years older than Julia.

If Sophia Hayden could be a successful architect, why not Julia?

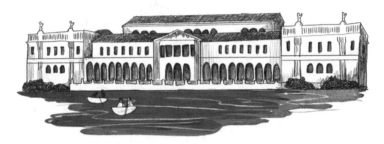

A female architect, Sophia Hayden, won a contest to design a Women's Building for the 1882 World's Fair.

Chapter 2
Julia Studies to be an Architect

In September 1890, Julia Morgan entered UC Berkeley. She was one of 450 students, of whom about 100 were women. She went to school on an Oakland Railroad Company streetcar. The streetcar ran along tracks and was horse-drawn. During her first year, Julia Morgan's parents insisted that her brother accompany her on the ride to school. Fortunately, Julia and her brother got along well. Since she was being allowed to pursue her college dream, Julia did not make a fuss about this arrangement.

Because UC Berkeley did not offer courses in architecture, her cousin's husband, Pierre LeBrun, suggested that Julia enroll in civil engineering. He believed it would provide her with some of the necessary background she would need in the future. This proved to be a very wise recommendation.

Julia's studies were difficult. She took classes in math, science, engineering, drawing, surveying, and astronomy. She learned to draw plans and to solve practical building problems. Sometimes she was the only woman in a class. Many of the male students resented her being there, but Julia persevered. She realized she had chosen a field few women had gone into before. She was also a pioneer in her family. Her sister, Emma, would decide two years later to follow in Julia's footsteps and also attend the UC Berkeley.

Emma Morgan followed in Julia's footsteps and attended college, eventually studying law before getting married.

Julia would later return to UC Berkeley to design a new Kappa Alpha Theta chapter house and headquarters for the sorority.

Julia joined the first sorority to form on campus, Kappa Alpha Theta. She didn't know it then, but many of her sorority sisters would grow into wealthy women. They would one day have Julia design their homes. During her college years, Julia met the wealthy widow, Phoebe Apperson Hearst. Phoebe had a home next to the campus and often invited young female students to come over for tea and conversation. The Hearst family would be a significant force in Julia's life as an architect.

Phoebe Hearst loved archaeology and funded many expeditions, resulting in her owning the largest collection of Egyptian antiquities west of the Mississippi River.

Phoebe Hearst was the widow of George Hearst. He made his money in mining and investing in silver, stocks, ranches, and timberland. He bought into several mines such as the Ophir Mine, the Ontario Silver Mine in Utah, the Homestake gold mine in South Dakota, and the Anaconda copper mine in Montana. George Hearst became a US senator, and died in office in 1891.

Phoebe Hearst enjoyed her wealth and position, and was sometimes referred to by members of the Hearst Corporation as the "Empress." She was a philanthropist, who gave money to countless causes, including UC Berkeley where she became its first woman regent.

Professor George Washington Percy of the College of Engineering helped to mentor Julia during her first three years at UC Berkeley. During her senior year, a young professor named Bernard Maybeck began to teach at UC Berkeley. Finding that there was no department of architecture and many students interested in this field, Maybeck began offering informal seminars in architecture to students at his home. Among this small group of students was Julia. This association with Maybeck was one of the most important and long-lasting that Julia would ever make.

Julia's graduating class did something unusual for their commencement ceremony. One of the students had discovered a natural semi-circular amphitheater at the bottom of the hills by the campus. For a podium for the ceremony, they used the stump of a large eucalyptus tree. The graduating students wore brown hooded gowns. During the ceremony, Julia played a violin solo. The site proved popular, and many future commencements were held there.

In the spring of 1894, Julia became the first woman to graduate with a Bachelor of Science degree in civil engineering from UC Berkeley. She went to work for Bernard Maybeck and studied drawing at the Hopkins School of Art Instruction. One of her first jobs while working for Maybeck was to design a house for Andrew Lawson, a geology professor at Berkeley.

Bernard Maybeck encouraged Julia to continue her studies at the same school that he had attended, the École nationale supérieure des Beaux-Arts in Paris. This school of fine arts was the most famous architecture school in the world. Its architecture division was founded in 1671.

So, in 1896 at age 24, Julia decided to go to Paris. First, she went to New York, which took almost a week. There she visited relatives including the architect Pierre LeBrun. Julia investigated the Polytechnic Institute in Cambridge, Massachusetts to see what course of studies they had. Then, traveling with a female cousin, Julia set off on her voyage across the ocean. She arrived in Paris on June 6, 1896. The two young women found rooms and, with letters of introduction, looked up family friends and relatives, as well as friends of Bernard Maybeck.

The trip from Oakland to Paris was 6,527 miles, or about 1/4 of the Earth's circumference.

Julia was determined to attend the École. She was soon faced with the difficult exams required to enter the school of architecture. Several hundred men took the exams each year, but only about forty were admitted. Up to this time, no woman had ever been admitted to study there. The exams included questions about design, engineering, and the history of architecture.

The buildings of the École were designed by Félix Duban, who graduated from the school in 1823.

Students at the École and those preparing to take the exams joined studios called ateliers. The ateliers were run by independent architects to instruct the students. Julia, along with ten

Bernard Maybeck was a mentor to Julia Morgan, and later worked with her on several projects.

others, joined the studio of Marcel de Monclos. Each student paid fees for the rent of the studio building and the costs of the instructor. At first, Julia mainly helped the more advanced students by adding color or minor details to their drawings. She also studied the history of architecture and design and worked to improve her French language skills.

In February 1897, her old friend and instructor Bernard Maybeck came to Paris with his wife Annie. Maybeck was in charge of an international architectural competition to design a new building program for UC Berkeley campus. Phoebe Apperson Hearst was financing this competition. In addition to a prize, the winner would also be asked to design several of the new campus buildings.

While he was in Paris, stirring up interest in the competition, Maybeck convinced school officials to allow Julia to take the entrance exams to study architecture at the École.

Still somewhat unfamiliar with the language and with converting measurements into the metric system, Julia made mistakes and did poorly on her exams in July. She re-took the exams in October and, although she did better, she was still not among the top few students and once again was not admitted. At the time, it was rumored that her exam had been graded more strictly than those of some of the men who took the exam. Some people did not want a female in the program.

The Ecole had all new students take a very difficult exam, and usually only the top 15% passed.

Another woman who had to overcome sexism in the architecture world, Henrietta Dozier was born in 1872, the same year as Julia, in Fernandina Beach, Florida. Her father died before she was born. Before she was two, Henrietta's mother moved the family to Atlanta. After graduating from high school, Dozier worked in an architect's office before attending the Pratt Institute in

Brooklyn, New York. Then she enrolled in the Massachusetts Institute of Technology (MIT) and earned her degree in architecture in 1899.

Dozier moved back to Atlanta, and was the first female architect in Georgia and the third female member of the American Institute of

Emma visited Avery and Julia in Europe
while they were studying to enter the École.

Architects. Among her buildings in Atlanta was an Episcopal Church and the Southern Ruralist Building. The latter was what she considered her best work. After working in the Atlanta area for thirteen years, she moved to Jacksonville, Florida, and opened an office there. Among her works

Henrietta Dozier designed many buildings, but some of them were under male names like H. C. Dozier or Harry Dozier.

were houses, apartment buildings, schools, churches, banks, and government buildings.

Henrietta Dozier consistently concealed the fact that she was a woman by referring to herself in writing as Harry or H. C. Dozier. She died in Jacksonville in 1947.

Fighting the sexism at the École, Julia began to study to re-take the exam. She developed eye problems from the strain. She also found a new teacher named Bernard Chaussemiche and joined a new study group. Her new instructor was encouraging, and this boosted Julia's spirits. Julia then took the examinations for a third time and was finally admitted in 1899. Her brother, Avery, came to Paris and began his studies to take the exams to enter the school as well. The two of them shared an apartment.

Phoebe Hearst also made a trip to Paris at about this time and stopped in to visit Julia. The two got along very well, and Hearst even offered financial help for Julia's studies. Julia assured her that help was not needed, but she was grateful to Phoebe for the offer.

During her 1901 travels around Europe,
Julia Morgan visited Notre Dame Cathedral.

While Julia was in Europe, Marion Griffin became the first licensed female architect in the United States. Marion Mahony was born in Chicago in 1871 and was graduated from the Massachusetts Institute of Technology in 1894. She was the second woman to graduate in architecture from MIT. When she received her architect's license from the state of Illinois in 1898, she became the first licensed female architect in the United States.

That same year, Marion went to work in the offices of Frank Lloyd Wright. She designed a few buildings of her own, but her acclaim came from the remarkable architectural drawings that she produced of other's work.

In 1911, Marion Mahony married another architect, Walter Burley Griffin, who worked in the same firm, mostly doing landscape architecture. The newly-weds set to work in creating designs for an international competition to plan Canberra, the new capital city of Australia. With the help of family and friends, they completed the plans and drawings and sent them by ship to Australia. They won the competition.

Marion and Walter Griffin went to Australia in 1914. He worked on Canberra until 1920 when they decided to live permanently in Australia. She worked in her husband's office, but Marion designed only one building in Australia under her own name. Occasionally they made trips back to the United States.

In 1935, Walter Griffin designed a library for the University of Lucknow in India and Marion Griffin joined him there in 1936. She worked in his office and continued making her remarkable architectural drawings. After Walter's death in 1937, Marion Griffin closed the office in India and returned to Australia. Shortly thereafter, she moved back to Illinois where she lived until 1961.

Julia Morgan couldn't be the first female architect in the United States, but she could still be the best. When she finally began her studies at the École, she was the first female student in the architecture section. Students who passed

Julia earned her degree by submitting a design for a palace-like theater, before heading back home to San Francisco.

the entrance exams became part of the Second Class. Second Class students attended lectures and entered monthly competitions. These monthly competitions might call for sketches or complete project plans. Points were earned for placing well in each of these competitions.

Once a student had earned sixteen points, the student became part of the First Class. Again there were competitions, but the assignments were more difficult. After accumulating another ten points, a student would achieve a certificate of graduation.

Julia completed many project drawings and entered competitions. She began to receive recognition for her good work. She was awarded many mentions and four medals for exceptional work in her designs and drawings. Julia even got a few paying jobs outside of school. But she knew that she was racing against time. The École did not allow students over thirty years old to accumulate points toward a certificate of graduation.

In the summer of 1901, Julia traveled around Europe sketching in Italy and Germany. Her brother often accompanied her on these trips. Finally, in December 1901, Julia became the first woman to receive the *certificat d'etude d'architecte*, the certificate of study in architecture. She had finished her studies in Paris less than a month before her thirtieth birthday. She had completed a five-year degree in only three years.

Julia sailed home to America early in 1902.

Chapter 3
Julia's Early Work in the Bay Area

Pierre LeBrun, Julia's cousin's husband, offered her a job in his architectural firm in New York. But after her training in France, Julia Morgan returned to California. She had been away for six years. San Francisco and the entire Bay Area were growing and many new buildings were going up. She hoped to design and build some of these.

Julia moved back into the old Oakland home with her parents. She found changes there, too. Her oldest brother, Parmalee, had married and moved away to southern California. Her youngest brother, Sam, had grown up. He opened a moving and storage company and eventually joined the Oakland Fire Department. Her sister, Emma, had attended law school in San Francisco and married a young lawyer named Hart North.

Julia's third brother, Avery, tried out a number of jobs. He was a charming young man with lots of interests, and he made friends easily. But his interests did not last long. He moved from one job to another and never really settled on a career.

Julia converted the carriage house behind her parents' Oakland home into a simple office. Friends and neighbors brought her a number of small commissions, mostly to design homes. Although Bernard Maybeck did not have work for her, he directed her to John Galen Howard. He was in charge of implementing the master building plan for the campus of the UC Berkeley. Phoebe Apperson Hearst, who was donating money for this building program, knew Julia and recommended the young architect. So Howard hired Julia to assist him in 1902.

Julia's first project on campus was to work on the team that designed the Hearst Mining Building. This building was to be a memorial to George Hearst, who had become wealthy through his investments in mining. The completed Hearst

Mining Building, with its white walls and red tile roof reminiscent of California missions, pleased Phoebe Hearst and she asked Galen Howard to find more work for Julia Morgan.

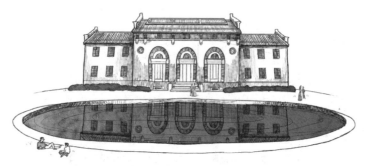

Originally, the Hearst Mining Building was designed to hold UC Berkeley's College of Mines. Completed in 1907, now it is home to a science and engineering department.

A former employee claimed to overhear a conversation Howard had with a friend where Howard commented that he liked his new assistant. He found her to be smart and hardworking.

Howard made Morgan his assistant supervising architect in building an outdoor theater on the UC Berkeley campus. The place chosen was the very site of Julia's graduation. The theater was to be shaped in a semicircle like the one in Epidaurus, Greece. The Greek

Theatre had to be ready in just a few months for the commencement in May 1903. The president of the United States, Teddy Roosevelt, was scheduled to speak.

In building the Greek Theatre on the University of California campus, Julia Morgan introduced the use of steel-reinforced concrete to UC Berkeley.

Morgan set right to work introducing her building staff to the idea of using reinforced concrete. Used in England and France, the technique of pouring concrete over steel bars for strength was not used commonly in the United States yet. Under Julia Morgan's direction, workers set about building a stage with columns and seats for 6,000 people.

William Randolph Hearst, Phoebe's son who had commissioned the project, met Julia Morgan when he came to look at the Greek

Theatre. William Randolph Hearst promised to have another project for the young architect sometime in the future.

The Greek Theatre project was technically still under construction. As President Roosevelt gave the graduation address, the concrete was still damp on the thick wall behind the stage. Banners were draped to conceal the drying concrete. Julia's reputation as an architect grew.

Although she was very pleased with her situation and enjoyed working in Howard's office, Julia decided it was time to leave and to set up her own independent practice. In 1904, Julia took the state examination for certification as an architect, passed, and became the first woman to be licensed as an architect in California.

Julia opened her architectural offices on Montgomery Street in San Francisco. Her junior partner was Ira Wilson Hoover, who had served as Galen Howard's chief draftsman until he left to join Julia's new practice in 1904. Hoover continued to work with her for the next six years.

Mary Colter's designs helped create the style that would be used for buildings throughout the National Parks.

Around the same time, another female architect was becoming famous in the Southwest United States. Mary Elizabeth Jane Colter was born in 1860 in Pittsburgh, Pennsylvania. Her family lived in Colorado and Texas before permanently settling in St. Paul, Minnesota.

After high school, Mary attended the California School of Design, now called the San Francisco Art Institute, graduating in 1910. When she apprenticed in an architectural firm, she learned about California mission style design.

Mary moved back to St. Paul, Minnesota. She taught art, drafting, and architecture for fifteen years in the high school and in University classes. She took a summer job with Fred Harvey Restaurants helping to decorate a hotel in Albuquerque, New Mexico. Mary began to work full-time as an interior decorator and as one of the Fred Harvey architects. Harvey's hotels and restaurants made use of staff anthropologists to offer appealing Native American arts, crafts, and décor to visitors.

Mary was assigned to do the interior design and decorating at the La Fonda hotel in Santa Fe. It became the most popular of the Harvey hotels. She hired artisans from local pueblos to make the hotel furniture. Native American designs were used in fixtures and decorations throughout the hotel.

Mary worked on a number of projects on the South Rim of the Grand Canyon including the 1905 Hopi House, the 1914 Hermit's Rest, the 1932 Desert View Watchtower, and the 1935 Bright Angel Lodge. Colter did not design, but she did decorate, the El Tovar Hotel.

Women still only make up 20% of licensed architects, but Julia tried to give other female architects as much help as she could.

The Harvey Company got permission to build and operate a camp on Bright Angel Creek at the bottom of the Grand Canyon. Mary used local natural materials to build Phantom Ranch.

In the years that followed, her work became a model for later projects in national parks.

Mary's favorite project was La Posada Hotel in Winslow, Arizona. She was the architect and designer for the entire resort. This included buildings, gardens, furniture, china, and staff uniforms. Toward the end of her career, she designed the Fred Harvey Restaurant in Union Station in Los Angeles. She retired to Santa Fe in 1948.

Unlike Mary Colter, Julia Morgan didn't teach in a school. However, once she opened her own architectural offices in San Francisco, Julia hired many young female architects and enabled them to get started in this male-dominated career.

Julia started off with small projects, mostly houses. At her new offices, she was commissioned for many small projects, mostly homes, throughout the state. Some were for former friends; others came as her reputation grew.

Julia was hired to remodel a large country home for Phoebe Hearst. This was followed by another big project: the design and building of a bell tower for the campus of Mills College. Mills College had received a group of ten bronze bells in 1902. The president of the college secured funds to build a bell tower in which to hang them. Julia was recommended for this commission by Phoebe Hearst

In 1904, the completed seventy-two foot-high bell tower had a red tile roof and concrete walls reinforced with steel. The trustees of Mills College were very impressed with Julia's work. When Margaret Carnegie donated funds the following year for a new library on the Mills College campus, Julia was commissioned to design it. And in 1909, she was again hired to design a gymnasium for the college.

In 1924, Julia built the Ming Quong Home for Chinese Girls on a two-acre site next to Mills College. It featured a square courtyard and became part of Mills College in 1936 where it served as a campus conference center. In 2004, it was renovated and became the Julia Morgan School for Girls, an all-girls middle school.

The bell tower at Mills College, designed by Julia Morgan, survived the 1989 earthquakes due to Julia using reinforced concrete to build it.

Julia never seemed to lack for work. She also always encouraged young women. She offered several female architects the opportunity to work in her offices and served as their mentor. She designed many YWCA buildings whose purpose was to offer security and places for young women to live while pursuing careers.

As an all-girls middle school, Julia Morgan School for Girls focuses on enabling students to realize their full potential.

Julia was designing and building from the Oregon border down to San Diego. She always interviewed clients herself and prepared preliminary drawings. Whenever she was faced with a building to design, Julia started with the building's interior design. She planned for each of the needed rooms, deciding upon their appropriate size and how they were to be placed in reference to other rooms. She also considered the height of ceilings and how rooms would be lit through windows. Morgan believed that rooms should be backdrops for the activities that took place in them. She closely supervised the development of final plans and inspected the work site.

Although trained in classical architecture, Julia integrated traditions from the American West into her work. Many of her contemporaries were also experimenting with new designs. The resulting style was called the Arts and Crafts movement, linked to the Arts and Crafts movement in England.

The climate and setting in northern California helped to blur the distinction between outdoors and indoors. Julia was open to new techniques and always practical in her use of form, space, and structure. She tried to create buildings that looked good in the landscape. Spectacular views were featured through large panes of glass, and native materials, like redwoods, were often used in construction.

Arthur De Wint Foote, engineer of the North Star Mines, needed somewhere to entertain guests, so he had Julia Morgan design a beautiful house near his mining complex.

Julia continued to see Bernard Maybeck. He too was experimenting with new designs. He tried putting support beams outside the houses that he built. Inside, these beams crisscrossed in an open attic area. Rather than being hidden, they were incorporated into the decor. In 1901, Phoebe Hearst commissioned Maybeck to build her a vacation home. It was on eighty square miles of forest she owned. Nearby was the McCloud River near the border of California and

Oregon. Maybeck hired Julia Morgan to be his assistant on the project.

Bernard Maybeck's original Wyntoon castle was designed to look like a German castle on the Rhine River.

Maybeck and Morgan designed and built a seven-story mansion that was made of local stone. The estate was called Wyntoon. This was the first, but not the last, castle that Julia Morgan would build. Phoebe Hearst loved Wyntoon when it was finished in 1904. On the strength of this excellent work, she decided on another project for Julia Morgan. Mrs. Hearst took Morgan with her to see an unfinished hunting lodge belonging to her family that was located on 2,000 acres of land not far from Oakland.

Phoebe Hearst explained that she wanted the old lodge remodeled into a house where she could hold large functions in connection with her charity work. The The newly renovated house was to be called La Hacienda del Pozo de Verona. It would include an Italian stone wellhead in the garden. Also to be included were guest houses and servant's quarters. The beautiful ninety-two-room complex in Pleasanton, California, took several years to complete.

La Hacienda del Pozo de Verona means The House of the Wellhead of Verona. A wellhead Phoebe Hearst found in Verona was the center of the project.

Chapter 4
After the San Francisco Earthquake

Although Julia Morgan's reputation was growing and many clients and other architects visited her new offices in San Francisco, John Galen Howard did not come. Perhaps he never forgave her for going out on her own and leaving his firm where she had done such good work for him. He probably was also unhappy that Julia had taken one of his good assistants, Ira Hoover, with her. Galen Howard used his influence to keep Julia from getting any more commissions at UC Berkeley for the next twenty-five years.

Julia continued to live in the family's home in Oakland while working out of her offices in San Francisco. At any given time, she was involved with many projects and had six to ten assistants working for her. She did not consider herself to be a feminist, but she did hire as many qualified women as she could.

Julia lived modestly, despite designing luxurious buildings.

Julia's routine of designing and building for Phoebe Hearst and many other clients was suddenly and dramatically interrupted. At 5:12 in the morning on Wednesday, April 18, 1906 while Julia was at home in bed, the famous San Francisco earthquake struck. The earthquake lasted forty seconds. Streets fractured, buildings came smashing down, gas lines broke, and fires blazed up everywhere in the Bay Area. Although dishes came crashing off the cupboards in the Morgan residence in Oakland, the house and people all survived.

Julia boarded a ferry boat at seven that morning and headed for San Francisco. She walked the several blocks to her work place. The Merchant Exchange building, which housed her offices, was still standing, but electricity was out, and small fires were burning nearby. Unable to do anything, she took the ferry back to Oakland. Later, the fires spread to the Merchant Exchange building, and it burned until only its outside walls remained standing. Although much was lost, many of Julia's architectural books that were stored at her Oakland home were spared.

Fire departments were almost helpless in the disaster. Their trucks and equipment had been damaged, streets were torn up, and water lines were broken. In San Francisco, the fire burned for days. When it finally was put out, the terrible damage could be assessed. About 700 people lost their lives, another 300,000 were homeless, and approximately 28,000 buildings were destroyed.

The damage to San Francisco cost over $400 million in 1906, or more than $10.9 billion now.

In addition to the disaster in San Francisco, there was earthquake damage in Berkeley, Oakland, and up and down the California coast. At Mills College, one of the classroom buildings crumbled, but the library and bell tower that Julia had designed withstood the quake. Morgan's idea to use reinforced concrete had proved to be a wise one.

One of the buildings damaged in the San Francisco earthquake was the new Fairmont Hotel. This 600-room building, perched up on Nob Hill in San Francisco, was nearly complete when the earthquake struck. The earthquake caused the structure to buckle. Then fires further damaged the building. Julia was commissioned to rebuild the structural work of the hotel. The owners wanted to reopen in a year.

Though the exterior of the building survived the earthquake, the interior and support beams were destroyed.

Julia worked with Ira Hoover out of temporary office space. Work on the Fairmont project began immediately, and Julia supervised every detail of the structural reconstruction. She personally examined the ruins carefully so that she could direct the replacement of beams and columns.

Julia seldom carried a purse with her because she found that purses got in her way. Instead, she stuffed everything into pockets. She fearlessly climbed scaffolds in her tailored dark suits, often wearing a pair of men's trousers beneath her long skirts. She inspected every aspect of the building, checked on all the work, and if it did not meet her standards, it was torn out.

As promised, just one year after the earthquake, the Fairmont Hotel opened in April 1907. There was a grand party, and some of the people who moved into the hotel were those who had lost their homes and apartments in the earthquake the year before. Her work on the renovation added to Julia's reputation as an important architect. Julia re-opened her own offices in the Merchant Exchange Building when it was rebuilt, and later on she helped with the remodeling of the interior of the building.

More than 13,000 oysters, 600 pounds of turtle, and $5,000 in wine were served at the Fairmont Hotel's grand opening.

In 1908, one of Julia's projects was to build a headquarters, near the UC Berkeley campus, for her old sorority, Kappa Alpha Theta. Much later, in 1930, she did a renovation on the building as well.

After the quake, Julia rebuilt the interior of the First Baptist Church in Oakland. A few years later, in 1910, she began building Saint John's Presbyterian Church in Berkeley. Because funds for the project were very limited, Julia had to design a simple structure that would fit in a residential block. She built it low to the ground and linked the church by a glass corridor to the Sunday School. She used exposed overhead beams and supports to give the interior the warm, rich color of wood. Light was admitted on all four sides through high, smoked glass windows.

Many of Julia's commissions were for buildings for the Young Women's Christian Association (YWCA). She was sympathetic to the goals of this and other organizations that were establishing headquarters, schools, living quarters, and hospitals for women and children. There was a shortage of housing for female workers moving into cities. Most earned less than a living wage, and YWCAs helped to meet their needs.

Julia designed and built sixteen buildings on the Asilomar grounds, including Merrill Hall, the last and largest building.

In 1912, Phoebe Hearst helped acquire thirty acres of coastal land near Monterey for a conference center for the YWCA. Phoebe Hearst suggested that Julia be given the commission to be the architect for what was called Asilomar, the refuge by the sea. This conference complex included a chapel, a dining room, an administration building, an auditorium, swimming pool, gymnasium, and dormitories.

The YWCA worked to help women and girls all over the world who were moving to cities and joining the work force.

Throughout the years that followed, Julia designed many more buildings for the YWCA throughout the state in cities like Berkeley, San Jose, Palo Alto, and San Diego. Her designs combined comfort, beauty, and practicality. One that she built in 1913 in Oakland featured a sunny interior courtyard.

Julia designed the YWCA building for the Panama-Pacific International Exposition of 1915 which was hosted by the City of San Francisco. In 1924, on a piece of this exposition land, she built The Heritage for the Ladies Protection and Relief Society to provide housing and permanent care for the elderly. Morgan did so many projects for the YWCA throughout the country that she was eventually asked to move to the Midwest and become their full-time architect. She declined.

Julia accumulated a huge library of books in her San Francisco office. Many of these were given to her by her cousin's husband, Pierre LeBrun, after he retired and closed his New York offices. Julia's office space also included a room with drafting tables, a bulletin board showing pictures of work under construction, and models of buildings. In this complex, she also had a small private office. Sometimes her friend, Maybeck, also used her office. Other employees such as engineers and crafts people worked out of the various building sites.

Throughout her career, Julia built in cities, foothills, and mountains. She thrived on all kinds of different projects including a Methodist Chinese Mission School in San Francisco, and many Arts & Crafts style houses that blended into their environment. Her houses were done in many different styles. She always tried to meet her client's wishes. She even built a warehouse for her brother's moving and storage business. In the twelve years after she returned to the Bay Area from Paris, Julia Morgan finished 300 commissions.

Large ferries were the only way to get to the mainland quickly before bridges were built across the bay.

By 1915, she had so many jobs going on at once in the Bay Area that she decided to buy an an automobile rather than to rely on ferry boats and trolleys. She hired her brother, Avery, to be her chauffeur and general helper. After another eight years, to save time, she began to fly to her various building projects.

Phoebe Hearst and other philanthropists gave money for all kinds of buildings, and Julia design-ed and built many of them. Most architects built two story elementary schools with staircases, but Julia was designing one- story school buildings. In her schools, each classroom opened directly to a courtyard or playground area.

Female architects were gaining ground across the country as well. When Pennsylvania began licensing architects in 1920, Anna Wagner Keichline became the first licensed architect in that state. Keichline was born in 1889 in Bellefonte, Pennsylvania. After graduating from high school in 1906, she studied mechanical engineering for one year at Pennsylvania State College where she was the only female in her class. She then studied at Cornell University to earn her architecture degree. She created buildings in Ohio; Washington, D.C.; and Pennsylvania.

In addition to being an architect, Keichline was an inventor and held six patents. One of these was for a specially shaped construction brick known as the "K-brick." Because she was fluent in German, Keichline served as a special agent in the Military Intelligence Division of the US Army during World War I. She died in 1943.

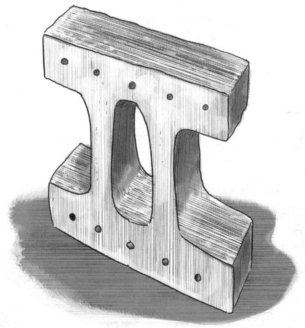

Anna Keichline's K brick led to the creation of modern cinderblocks. The hollow bricks were lighter and cheaper than solid bricks, while still being strong.

Marion Manley became a licensed architect in Florida and opened an office in 1924. Manley was born in 1893 in Junction City, Kansas. She was graduated from the University of Illinois in 1917 with a degree in architecture. When her brother began working in Miami, he encouraged her to move there. In a sixty-year career, she designed and built more than a hundred houses and commercial buildings.

William Randolph Hearst was a US representative in addition to owning a newspaper empire.

Among her accomplishments are several buildings on the campus of the University of Miami, as well as Miami's Post Office and Federal Building.

Some major changes for Julia came at the end of the 1910s. In 1919, her benefactress, Phoebe Apperson Hearst, died. Phoebe's Hearst's son William Randolph Hearst had come west from New York to be with his ailing mother. He had met Julia Morgan on previous trips to California. Only a month after his mother's death, William Randolph Hearst came to Julia Morgan's office in San Francisco. Hearst wanted Morgan to build him a lodge on a hill at San Simeon, California, where the family owned land.

This idea of a small bungalow to be built on top of a hill overlooking the Pacific Ocean eventually grew into a castle that Julia Morgan would be working on for the next twenty-eight years.

Chapter 5

Julia Morgan Builds a Castle at San Simeon

William Randolph Hearst went to see Julia Morgan in her San Francisco offices in 1919. He explained that he wanted her to build him a vacation house near San Simeon on ranchland that his father had purchased in 1865.

San Simeon is located on the California coast about midway between San Francisco and Los Angeles, 250 miles in either direction. William Randolph Hearst had camped there with his parents as a child, and brought his wife and five sons to camp as an adult. Instead of always roughing it, Hearst felt he was ready to have a comfortable house for vacations built there.

William Randolph Hearst certainly had the money to build anything he wished. On her death, Phoebe Hearst left William Randolph Hearst much of the money and land that her husband George had acquired. In addition to his inheritance, William Randolph Hearst had added to the Hearst wealth with money he had earned through building up a newspaper empire. His father gave him the *San Francisco Examiner* in 1887. He gradually acquired several others papers including the *Los Angeles Examiner*.

Hearst had started out requesting a lodge,
but the project evolved into an estate featuring
56 bedrooms and 61 bathrooms on 127 acres.

Hearst, one of the wealthiest men in the world, also inherited his mother's collection of paintings, statues, and tapestries. Some of this art can be seen at Hearst Castle today. If indeed Hearst ever planned to build a simple lodge at San Simeon, he quickly gave up that idea. And just as quickly, Julia realized that instead of designing a vacation bungalow at San Simeon, she was really being asked to build much more.

The San Simeon project along with all the other projects she was working on was a tremendous work load for Julia. Once the San Simeon project was underway, she continued to work in her office in San Francisco during weekdays. One weekend a month, she left her office on Friday afternoon and traveled more than 225 miles to San Luis Obispo by train. From there, she took a fifty-mile taxi ride to San Simeon. The same taxi company took her every week. In fact, Julia got to know one driver so well, she eventually designed a playhouse for the driver's little girl.

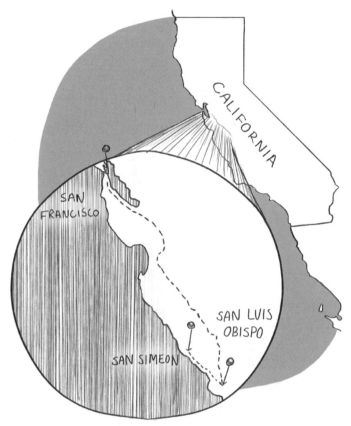

Julia made the 275 mile trip to San Simeon
many times during the next 20 years.

Julia would work at San Simeon until Sunday
night, and then go back to her office via taxi
and train the same way she had come. While at
San Simeon, she sometimes met with Hearst,
listened to what he wanted, and drew designs.
When Hearst was away, he sent her detailed

letters suggesting countless ideas for the project. Julia saw her job as one of bringing her client's dream to reality. Hearst made it clear that one of the most important things to be considered at San Simeon was the wonderful view from the top of this hill. He could see the Pacific Ocean, the coastline, and the surrounding hills.

Julia drew up plans for a main house where the Hearst family would stay while visiting the property, three guest houses, a rose garden, and a pool. All of these had wonderful hilltop views. Hearst wanted everything to be linked together by walks and gardens. Hearst gave this spot a Spanish name, La Cuesta Encantada, the Enchanted Hill. In speaking of this place, however, he simply called it "the ranch." Today, many people call it Hearst Castle.

One of the first things Julia had to do was transform a winding five mile path into a road from the shore of San Simeon up to the building site. A wharf had been built to handle sea shipments. Horses, wagons, and trucks were used to move building supplies and art treasures up the hill to the building site. Warehouses previously built by George Hearst were used by William Randolph Hearst to store things until they were needed on the build site. All kinds of workmen were hired, and they all reported to Julia. She held them to a very high standard of work.

Both Julia and Hearst were recognizable on-site by their hats. Hearst wore a straw boater while Julia wore a felt cloche hat.

At first, the laborers lived in tents at San Simeon, but Julia eventually built simple group cabins for them near the warehouses and at the top of the hill. For a few of the most important workers and their families, she built individual houses in the village. Erecting the buildings at San Simeon was hard work. Sometimes workmen finished a project only to see it torn out and rebuilt in a slightly different way because Hearst had come up with a "new idea." This discouraged workers, and some of them quit. In order to try to keep her workmen happy, Julia hired a cook that they liked to prepare their meals and even arranged for a movie to be shown each week for entertainment.

In this telegraph, Hearst declared the bathrooms of the guest houses to be "narrow, dark, and uncomfortable."

Over the next few years, wherever he was, Hearst kept in touch with Julia and her progress at San Simeon. He continued to send her letters and telegrams suggesting ideas and changes for his house. Most of the ideas were his own, but some were from his wife. These messages numbered in the thousands. Sometimes there were letters of complaint, but he was always respectful, and sometimes funny! One time when he felt that the chimney was not working properly in the main house, Hearst wrote to Julia, "We have the unsatisfying alternative of freezing to death without a fire, or smothering to death from smoke." On another occasion, Hearst expressed his opinion about the Great Hall, writing, "The wind flows in through the cracks and the crevices until the rugs flap on the floors."

Hearst bought art and antiques at auctions and galleries. His agents helped him search out other art treasures. And he sent most of these to his new home at San Simeon. It would be up to Julia to decide how to incorporate these into the new house. Sometimes Julia recommended what should be bought.

The first completed building at San Simeon was Casa del Monte.

The three guest houses, which were placed slightly lower than the main house so as not to obstruct the view, were built first. Julia was closely involved in the supervision of the construction, often walking out on scaffolding to get a good look. Unfortunately for Julia and the construction crew, Hearst continued to change his mind frequently. He once had a fireplace torn out after it was built only to have it torn out again and put back exactly where it was originally. For Hearst, it seemed that tearing down was a natural part of building perfection. Julia, continuing with her long held belief that her job was to please the client, put up with all these changes and suggestions.

Each of the three guest houses at San Simeon was given a Spanish name. Casa del Mar had a view of the sea, Casa del Monte had a view of the mountains, and Casa del Sol faced the setting sun. These houses were built in Spanish style with white walls and red tile roofs. Each contained four to eight bedrooms and a grand sitting room. Each was elaborately furnished. These small houses had no dining rooms, just

Casa del Sol was designed to have beautiful views of the sunset.

bedrooms and sitting rooms. Guests ate with their host in the main building. Hearst and his family stayed in Casa del Mar when they visited the construction site.

On a visit to Europe before his mother's death, William Randolph Hearst fell in love with the tower of the cathedral in Ronda, Spain.

Casa del Monte was ready for Hearst and his family to use in the summer of 1921. By 1924, all three guests houses were completed, and construction had begun on the main house which was called La Casa Grande, the big house. They decided on a tower for this building based on the Gothic Cathedral of Santa Maria in Ronda, Spain. This was soon expanded to two towers.

Though the dining hall was decorated to look like a medieval dining hall, every table had ketchup and mustard bottles to remind guests they were on a ranch.

When Morgan thought that the main house was nearly finished, Hearst suddenly asked that they add another story. As always, Julia complied with her client's wishes. By 1926, although the main house was not complete, a suite of rooms in it was finished and Hearst stayed there on his visits later.

From his original request of a "lodge" on a hill, something else had grown. There are 115 rooms in the main building and guesthouses. There are thirty-eight bedrooms, forty-five baths, eighteen sitting rooms, and two libraries. Most are furnished with antiques and valuable objects of art.

Hearst used La Casa Grande to entertain in high style. His guests called him "The Chief" and were happy for an invitation to visit "the ranch." Floodlights lit up the building, so that as guests walked up the hill, it looked as if they were approaching a fairytale castle. Guests included such well known people as President Calvin Coolidge, Winston Churchill, Cary Grant, Clark Gable, Amelia Earhart, and Greta Garbo. And occasionally, Julia Morgan dined there and sat directly across the table from her host.

In addition to the buildings and the formal gardens, Julia was in charge of the design for the surrounding land. There was an orchard, vegetable gardens, and a poultry farm to supply his guests with fresh food. None of this was easy to achieve on a rocky hillside. Sometimes holes had to be blasted in rock and filled with soil before a fruit or pine tree could be planted.

The outdoor pool, the Neptune Pool, holds 345,000 gallons of water.

Hearst was always buying something new for San Simeon. Hearst had the idea of building a Roman temple near a swimming pool. Julia built what many consider to be the most beautiful swimming pool in the world, the Neptune Pool. Because it had to be built on a steep hillside, Morgan had to first support it with concrete beams and a concrete retaining wall. The pool was lined in white marble. At the end stood a replica Roman temple built from pieces of old castles and monasteries Hearst had purchased.

This pool proved so popular with guests that Hearst then asked that a second pool be built. This time, Julia designed and built an indoor pool lined with blue and gold Italian glass tiles. She located it beneath the tennis courts.

Marianne the elephant was a favorite at Hearst's zoo.
Julia was very thoughtful when designing her pen
so that she'd be comfortable.

In 1924, Hearst acquired forty buffalo from Montana and announced that he wanted a zoo at San Simeon. Julia designed enclosures for the animals. Signs on the estate said, "Animals Have Right of Way." By 1939, Hearst had given or sold his wild animals to the San Diego, San Francisco, and other zoos. Smaller animals, such as Barbary sheep and zebras, remained to roam on the ranchland.

William Randolph Hearst had a special bond with his dachshunds, especially Helen, who he took with him on his travels to Wyntoon, San Simeon, and the San Francisco bay area.

Hearst also had an interest in smaller animals. He kept fifty dachshund dogs in a kennel which Julia Morgan designed. A favorite dog, named

Helen, mingled with the guests in the Big House. Hearst also had a soft spot for all animals. He ordered his household staff to set non-lethal traps to catch mice, and then the mice were set free outdoors the next morning. One mouse visited so often that Hearst said he recognized it and nick-named the mouse Mortimer.

Although Hearst had continuing plans for San Simeon, expenses were high and Hearst sometimes ran low on funds. As he grew older and in poor health, Hearst Corporation executives were unwilling to continue to spend it on San Simeon.

When the building accounts for San Simeon were finally closed in 1945, the north and south wings of the main building were still unfinished. Ideas to build an English-style cottage and a Chinese-style cottage never materialized. Hearst left San Simeon for the last time in 1947, leaving only a skeleton crew of maintenance workers to stay on.

Chapter 6
The Unbuilt Castle
at Wyntoon

In addition to his magnificent castle at San Simeon, and while building was still going on there, William Randolph Hearst had plans for yet another castle in California. The lovely seven-story stone Gothic castle at Wyntoon, which had been designed in 1902 for Phoebe Hearst by Bernard Maybeck with Julia Morgan's assistance, burned to the ground in 1930.

This was one of the few properties William Randolph Hearst did not inherit upon his mother's death. Instead, his cousin Anne Flint inherited it. Hearst was angered about this and fought with his cousin about it until 1925 when he bought Wyntoon from Flint. Hearst was used to getting his way. He never forgave his cousin for keeping Wyntoon from him. He and his family had enjoyed summer visits to this area both before and after the death of Phoebe Hearst.

So although San Simeon was far from finished, Hearst decided that he wanted a castle at Wyntoon to be rebuilt, and he wanted Bernard Maybeck and Julia Morgan to build it.

Three artists worked on the exterior at Wyntoon: wood-carver Jules Suppo, painter Doris Day, and illustrator Willy Pogany.

Maybeck and Julia made drawings and a model for the new castle. These drawings show a medieval-looking castle that boasted two main towers, eight floors, and sixty-one bedrooms. Hearst could see that the cost of building a castle at Wyntoon and the castle at San Simeon at the same time was too high.

Julia came up with an alternate plan. She visited Austria and Bavaria in 1932 to gather ideas for this new project. On her return, Julia began to design Hearst's Bavarian-style village. She planned three separate, three-story cottages, each containing four to eight bedrooms, each with its own bathroom. Each cottage would be placed with its back to a river in a clearing in the middle of the forest, and eventually a castle could be built in their midst.

Dining and entertainment would be offered in a separate building called the Bend, at a bend in

The Gables served as both a dining house and a theater for Hearst to show his movies.

the McCloud River. River House, which had been built before 1900 on nearby property bought by Phoebe Hearst, was remodeled by Julia into an additional guest house. Bridge House, a wooden building with a tower, included a library and sitting rooms. The Gables, with a huge dining room, was completed in 1937, but was lost in a fire in 1945.

Julia also included in the plans for Wyntoon a swimming pool, tennis courts, croquet courts, and a tea house with boat landing. After the pool was built, a deck near the pool was filled with sand, two to three feet deep, to provide guests with a place for sun-bathing.

Each guest house looked like a small castle. Morgan used local stone and wood with steep roofs and many gables and chimneys. Artisans were brought in to paint murals and to carve sculptures from wood. One guest house was named Cinderella House. A second, often called Bear House, was also known as Snow White Rose Red, but not for long. And one house was alternately called Angel, Sleeping Beauty, or Fairy house. Ultimately, Angel House was the preferred name. The Cinderella and Bear houses had scenes from Grimm's fairytales painted on their outside. The third house was left undecorated and not finished inside until many years after Hearst died.

Though not the castle originally intended, Wyntoon could still house 100 people, filling all three guest houses.

Bear House, which had paintings of Snow White and Rose Red on its exterior, was used by William Randolph Hearst. He lived there one winter during World War II because living at Wyntoon was less costly than staying as San Simeon.

Bear House had a ornately carved wooden door and a stairway that curved up into a tower. It contained sixteenth-century Austrian fireplaces. Outside sat a sculptured stone fountain with a bear and a cub in the center. Next to Bear House, Morgan put a modest lodge which served as the newspaper headquarters while Hearst lived there.

Cinderella House had an exterior featuring the Cinderella story. It was built with a high-ceilinged living room to accommodate social gatherings. In the third house, which was never finished, Hearst stored some of his collection of Germanic art that wasn't on display.

The main house, or castle, which was to sit in the midst of this fairytale Bavarian village, was never built. Julia Morgan's involvement at Wyntoon spanned from 1924 to the 1940's. During much of this time, she traveled to Wyntoon one weekend a month while continuing to go to San Simeon one weekend month, and to work on her other projects during weekdays.

On one of her working weekends at Wyntoon, Julia suffered an accident that could easily have taken her life. Because of many problems and operations on her ear, Julia suffered some balance problems. She had never had a fear of heights and often climbed out on scaffolding to view work in progress. While supervising work at Wyntoon and ignoring her impaired balance, Julia fell from a scaffolding into an open water flume and went down it like a water slide. She was rescued from the other end wet and bruised, but not seriously hurt.

Between 1937 and 1943, the Hearst Corporation was restructured. Wyntoon lost its funding, and building stopped.

Julia enjoyed playing with her niece and nephew, Judith and
Morgan North. She even designed a playhouse for them.

Chapter 7
Julia Morgan's Later Years

During the time that she worked on San Simeon and Wyntoon, Julia took on many other jobs in her office. She also found time to help care for various needs of her family. Her sister, Emma, was married and lived nearby in Berkeley with her husband and three children. Julia's brother Parmalee had died in 1918, and her brother Gardiner was killed in an accident at age thirty-two. Julia's third brother, Avery, lived at home and helped care for their parents.

Since Julia never married and for many years lived with her parents, her family was very important to her. She provided and received emotional support from them. She was always very close to her sister and her sister's children.

When their father grew ill, Avery provided the needed nursing care until he died in 1924. Afterward, Avery had a nervous breakdown, and Julia took care of Avery. This is when she hired him to do odd jobs around the office and bought a car so that Avery could chauffeur her to various building sites.

In the mid-1920s, Julia bought two adjoining houses in San Francisco, re-modeled them into apartments, and lived in one of these apartments. She took a kindly interest in the other women who lived in her building. Julia's mother continued to live in the family home in Oakland and refused to move in with either of her daughters. To deal with this situation, Julia and her sister Emma came up with a plan.

While working on San Simeon for Hearst, Julia found time to remodel two apartment buildings for herself.

In 1909, Julia designed the house in Berkeley where Emma and her husband and their three children lived. There was room on the lot for a cottage, so in the 1920s, when her mother's health was not good, Julia Morgan designed and built a small cottage right next door to Emma's home. Julia designed the bedroom of this cottage so that it was an exact copy of her mother's room in the Oakland house.

On Thanksgiving Day, Julia's mother Eliza was invited to a family dinner at Emma's house. After dinner, instead of taking their mother home, her children took Eliza to the cottage next door. When she went to her bedroom and found all of her things exactly as they were in her old home, Eliza was content to live there. Emma visited her mother daily, and she supervised the nurses until Eliza Morgan died in 1929.

In the same year as her mother's death, Julia Morgan received a special honor. She accepted the honorary degree of Doctor of Laws from UC Berkeley at a graduation ceremony. In part, her degree read, "Architect, in whose work harmony and admirable proportions bring pleasure to the eye and peace of mind."

Although San Simeon took up much of Julia Morgan's time, she continued to build for the YWCA. She designed the Sausalito Women's Club, and in 1922 built the Studio Club in Hollywood.

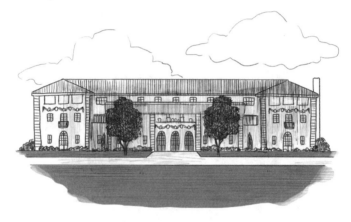

The Studio Club in Hollywood that Julia Morgan designed is now used as a digital learning academy by the YWCA.

As a memorial to his mother, Phoebe Hearst, William Randolph Hearst had Julia and her old friend Bernard Maybeck design the Phoebe Apperson Hearst Gymnasium at UC Berkeley in 1925. Part of the spur for this building was the fact that a previous gym and social center,

Hearst Hall, burned 1922. This earlier building had been designed by Maybeck.

The Hearst Memorial Gym included two gyms, three dance studios, and three outdoor swimming pools.

For the new gymnasium, William Randolph Hearst, hired both Maybeck and Morgan.

The building had not only athletic facilities but also contained rooms for lounging and sleeping to accommodate female students who might be traveling a considerable distance to attend school.

It contained three swimming pools that required 325,000 gallons of water. To handle the needs of the pools, the city of Berkeley built a new water treatment plant on Bancroft Way. When the Hearst Memorial Gymnasium opened, it was considered by many to be the most modern and lavish gym for women in the country.

In 1929, the Women's City Club in Berkeley hired Julia to design a building on land next door to their existing building. It was to house their educational and recreational facilities. In addition to building a ballroom, theater, and meeting rooms, Julia Morgan included a 1,875 square foot swimming pool. It was the only pool in Berkeley at that time that was open for year-round recreational swimming. The entire building was centered around two interior courts, filled with flowers and greenery that provided wells of light.

The Women's City Club of Berkeley began
accepting male membership in 1963
and is known today as the Berkeley City Club.

Julia also faced a health problem of her
own. As a child, she had a cold and serious
ear infection. In 1932, Julia had an emergency
surgery, which removed her inner ear. During the
surgery, the doctor accidentally severed a facial
muscle. This made Julia's face sag slightly on
one side.

Julia's doctor was so sorry for this slip during
the operation that he refused to take money for
the surgery and apologized over and over again.

Julia understood that it was simply an accident and forgave him. The doctor's wife loved orchids, and, knowing that, Julia sent flowers to his wife every year for Christmas.

It was this operation on her ear that affected her sense of balance. In spite of this, she continued to work, but was shyer than ever and seldom went out.

Many weekends, Julia continued to supervise the ongoing building at San Simeon and Wyntoon. She also worked on a number of commercial commissions for the Hearsts. In 1937, she did a major renovation of the Hearst Building in San Francisco. This included adding a marble lobby and a radio broadcasting studio.

Hearst continued to have other grand building plans. One of these was to build Babicora Hacienda in northwestern Mexico. Julia Morgan made several trips to Mexico City and to Babicora to look into building materials. Then there was talk of the Mexican government taking property held by foreigners. So the Babicora Hacienda project was indefinitely postponed in June 1944.

Although William Randolph Hearst never ran out of plans, he did run out of support from the Hearst Corporation. The trustees slowly stopped funding his building projects. Work at San Simeon stopped in the late 1930s, beginning again in 1943. Julia continued to work on Wyntoon into the 1940s.

In these later years, Julia began to travel more. Late in 1947, she took a five month trip to South America. The next year, she visited Europe. Although well enough to take buses and walk miles on foot to visit many towns and admire buildings, she was also suffering instances of severe memory loss. Since her seventy-fifth birthday, Julia had been aware that she was suffering memory loss, and it frustrated and angered her.

Poor health eventually caused William Randolph Hearst to move to Beverly Hills, California to be closer to his doctors. He died in 1951 at the age of eighty-eight. The year before, Julia had finally decided to close her offices. Julia wrote to all of her clients to inform them of her decision to close her offices in San Francisco and gave them a period of time in which to contact her to get copies of anything she had that might be of interest to them. After this time period, it was believed she had most of her architectural plans and business papers destroyed. Instead, her secretary stored many of them in her garage. Julia did keep her letters and telegrams from Hearst which are now in California Polytechnic State University, San Luis Obispo archives. Beginning in 1951, Julia began to have minor strokes. She had a nurse-companion for the

From when her offices opened in 1904 and when they closed in 1950, Julia designed and built more than 700 buildings.

last four years of her life and seldom left her apartment in San Francisco. Julia Morgan died on February 2, 1957 at age eighty-five.

In 1958, the state of California accepted the San Simeon property from the Hearst Corporation and family as a memorial to Phoebe Apperson Hearst and her son, William Randolph Hearst. It is now called the Hearst San Simeon State Historical Monument and is operated by California State Parks. It opened to the public in 1958. Each year, hundreds of thousands of visitors tour the buildings and grounds.

Asilomar, designed by Julia Morgan, is one of the largest institutional complexes to be built in the Arts and Crafts style. It was designated a California State Monument in 1958 and is used as a conference center.

Julia Morgan's memorials are the more than 700 structures that she designed and built during her career. These include clubs, houses, schools, YWCA's, hospitals, a bell tower, and a Greek Theatre. They also include the castle she built for William Randolph Hearst at San Simeon which continues to enchant visitors year after year.

Select Quotes from
<u>Julia Morgan</u>

"Architecture is a visual art, and the buildings speak for themselves."

"Never turn down a job because it's too small; you don't know where it can lead."

Julia Morgan Timeline

1867   Bill Morgan comes to San Francisco

1868   Bill Morgan marries Eliza Parmalee

1872   Julia Morgan born in San Francisco

1872   The Morgans buy a lot to build their home in Oakland

1879   Julia gets a cold and an ear infection that troubles her throughout life

1890   Julia Morgan enrolls in UC Berkeley

1894   Julia Morgan meets Bernard Maybeck

1894   Julia Morgan graduates with degree in civil engineering from UC Berkeley

1901   Julia Morgan graduates from the École nationale supérieure des Beaux-Arts with degree in architecture

1903   Works on architectural team that builds Greek Theatre, UC Berkeley

1904   First woman licensed as architect in state of California

1904   Builds Bell Tower at Mills College, Oakland

1904   Julia Morgan opens her own architectural office in San Francisco

1906   San Francisco earthquake destroys Morgan's office

1907   Morgan rebuilds Fairmont Hotel after earthquake damage

1912   Julia Morgan begins building YWCA conference Center at Asilomar

1919   Begins to discuss with William Randolph Hearst

World Timeline

1848   Gold discovered at Sutter's Mill, California

1850   California becomes a state

1869   Transcontinental Railroad opens

1871   The Great Chicago Fire

1876   First telephone call was made by Alexander Graham Bell

1881   The assassination of President James A. Garfield

1883   The Brooklyn Bridge opens

1886   The Statue of Liberty is dedicated

1889   Johnstown, Pennsylvania flood

1898   Spanish-American War begins

1900   Galveston, Texas flood occurs

1903   Henry Ford sells first Model A auto

1903   First airplane flight by Orville and Wilbur Wright

1906   San Francisco earthquake and fire

1914   Panama Canal opens

1917   US enters World War I

1920   First US commercial radio broadcast

1928   First commercially licensed TV station opens in US

Julia Morgan Timeline (cont.)

the building of San Simeon

1924-1943   Worked on Wyntoon cottages

1925   Builds Phoebe Hearst Memorial Gymnasium on UC Berkeley campus

1929   Builds Berkeley Women's City Club

1948   San Simeon accounts closed although work is not finished

1950   Julia Morgan closes her San Francisco office

1957   Julia Morgan dies

World Timeline (cont.)

1929-1939 The Great Depression

1931 Empire State Building completed

1932 Kidnapping of Charles Augustus Lindbergh, Jr.

1936 San Francisco – Oakland Bay Bridge opens

1937 Golden Gate Bridge opens

1941 U.S. enters World War II

1946 First session of the United Nations is held

Glossary

Amphitheater   A building or theater with rising curved rows of seats around a lowered central stage

Architect   A person who designs buildings and supervises their construction.

Atelier   The studio or workshop of an artist or designer, french

Bavarian   Relating to the southeast region of Germany

Benefactor   Someone who helps someone else, especially by giving them money

Campus   The land and buildings of a university

Carriage House   A building used to store carriages; similar to a garage

Commission   An order to make, design, or build something

Drafting   Creating a sketch or outline of the building's design

Engineering   The design and creation of complex products

Exposition   A public exhibit or show

Gables   a triangular part of a building, like what is over a door or window

Inheritance   Possessions that are handed down through generations, usually after a death

Letter of Introduction   A letter used during the Victorian era to introduce two people, usually written by a mutual friend

Living Wage   A pay rate that is high enough to cover the cost of necessities like food, clothing, and shelter

Persist   To continue doing something even though it is difficult

Philanthropy   The act of caring about people, animals, or institutions, usually expressed through generous acts of kindness or charity

Regent   A member of a governing board who rules over a place or organization

Renovation   A restoration, modernization, or return to a better state, usually by cleaning, repairing, or rebuilding

Residential   Relating to places where people live

Scaffold   A supporting framework for workmen or craftsmen to stand on to reach high locations on a building

Seminar   A meeting for discussing information, especially by a group of advanced students

Skeleton Crew   The minimum number of people needed to do a job

Sorority   An organization of women usually formed for social purposes with Greek lettered names

Transcontinental   Refers to anything that goes across a continent

Victorian   Relating to the reign of Queen Victoria, 1837 to 1901

Wellhead   The structure built around or over a well, sometimes a fountain

Wharf   A structure built on a shore so that boats can load or unload cargo

Bibliography

Boutelle, Sara Holmes. *Julia Morgan, Architect*. New York: Abbeville Press, 1988.

James, Cary. *Julia Morgan, Architect*. New York, NY: Chelsea House Publishers, 1990.

Kastner, Victoria. *Hearst Castle: The Biography of a Country House*. New York: Harry N. Abrams, Inc. 2000

Longstreth, Richard W. *Julia Morgan, Architect*. Berkeley, CA: Berkeley Architectural Heritage Association, 1977.

Richey, Elinor. *Eminent Women of the West*. Berkeley, CA: Howell-North Books, 1975.

Wilson, Mark A. *Julia Morgan; Architect of Beauty*. Layton, Utah., Gibbs Smith Publishing, 2012.

Wadsworth, Ginger. *Julia Morgan, Architect of Dreams*. Minneapolis, MN: Lerner Publications, 1990.

Further Reading

Aidala, Thomas. *Hearst Castle, San Simeon*. New York: Hudson Hills Press, 1981.

Beach, John. *Architectural Drawings by Julia Morgan: Beaux-Arts Assignments and Other Buildings*. Oakland: The Oakland Museum Art Department, 1976.

Coffman, Taylor. *Hearst Castle, The Story of William Randolph Hearst and San Simeon*. Santa Barbara, CA: Sequoia Communications, 1985.

Longstreth, Richard. *On the Edge of the World: Four Architects in San Francisco at the Turn of the Century*. Cambridge, MA: MIT Press, 1993.

Macaulay, David, *Castle*. Boston: Houghton Mifflin, 1977.

Index

Index (cont.)

Index (cont.)

Index (cont.)

Index (cont.)

Index (cont.)

Index (cont.)

Index (cont.)

Index (cont.)

Index (cont.)